Songs of Kiguli: International Edition

Kiguli Army Primary School
Nakasongola, Uganda

Robinswood Middle School
Orlando, Florida, USA

Compiled and Edited by:
Citron Concasse', LLC
Aberdeen, Washington, USA

Copyright © 2017 by Kiguli Army Primary School

All rights Reserved. Published in the United States by Citron Concasse', LLC for the benefit of the Kiguli Army Primary School. No part of this book may be reproduced or transmitted in any form or by any means, electronic or mechanical, including photocopying, recording, or by information storage and retrieval systems without written permission of the Publisher with exceptions as to brief quotes, references, articles, reviews, and certain other noncommercial uses permitted by copyright law.

PERMISSIONS

For permission requests, write to Philip Matogo c/o 210 Hirschbeck Heights, Aberdeen, WA, USA.

PRINTING HISTORY
First Edition
August 2017

ISBN: 978-0-692-91920-0

Cover Design by Matt Ostrom

Dedication

Hello, poetry lovers and friends of humanity.

Songs of Kiguli is back and breathing. It feels good to be back after a short hiatus.

Poetry struck gold in the depths of the Ugandan wilderness when rural children started writing and publishing their poetry in the form of *Songs of Kiguli*. This reality captured the experiences of children on the margins of Ugandan society. Children who for so long had been denied a voice by the very experiences which they came to capture in *Songs of Kiguli*.

To be sure, with passion and poetry, they rose above their origins to chart horizons new. I was their teacher but their inspiration was Lisa McKinney. This lady personifies love and reflects in her heart the love that has come to embody *Songs of Kiguli*. We met online, two different people from two different worlds. She posted poetry that was sassy and self-confident. While I felt my way forth with an uncertainty that told in my poetry. I was unsure of myself but she was sure of me.

Her assurance was enough for every pronoun that was me, myself and I.

Although she was better written than I, she treated me as an equal. This helped my poetic wings unfurl. Then one day, I decided to post poems from the Kiguli Army Primary School's poetry club. Lisa (also fondly known as Nessa) immediately approached me with a proposition. "How would your children like to have their poems published?" she asked. I didn't believe what she was offering. Still, I jumped at the chance and, in a matter of months, *Songs of Kiguli* was available online and in bookshops in Uganda and the USA. Lisa was as good as her word.

She didn't charge us a coin.

Thereafter, *Songs of Kiguli* had a sequel. Then a third book which involved various collaborators like Uganda's premier music band, *Qwela*.

Songs of Kiguli had arrived and its story was inextricably tied up with the story of Lisa McKinney.

A lady who believed, as the children of Kiguli do, that God is the author of the life we co-author with poetry. I've said it before and I will say it again: Lisa is our guiding star.

If she wasn't married to the equally inspirational Todd McKinney, I would put forth my "manifesto," as we say in Uganda. That manifesto would have stated boldly and clearly: Lisa, you are one of a kind by being so kind as to be the one.

The one we look up to and love eternally. Thank you for the music that is Songs of Kiguli.

Philip Matogo, Teacher
Kiguli Army Primary School
Nakasongola, Uganda

Thank you for working diligently to help with compiling student work from across the globe. You have inspired a new generation of poets, while allowing these children the opportunity to explore common humanity. Learning about other's experiences and perspectives also helps them become more open-minded. The world will become a better place as these students explore creative ways to express themselves. We can't thank you enough for your time and patience.

Cindy Camp, Language Arts Teacher
Robinswood Middle School
Orlando, Florida, USA

Table of Contents

Acknowledgements

Our family, friends, and those we choose to love…

How we stay healthy, get well, and how we die…

Earth, wind, water, and fire…

Our climate, our seasons…

Cars, and trains, and planes…

The things we grow and raise, the things we eat…

How we learn, how we build knowledge…

How we communicate, our technology…

Our cultures, our country, and our society…

How we celebrate…

How we have fun, the arts of our people…

How we see faith, spirituality, ourselves, and others…

Acknowledgements

A project such as this takes commitments of time and talent. There are a number of folks that have contributed to the Kiguli poetry project over the years. These included people editing, formatting, designing, compiling, and just plain getting information and copy from one place to another. It is a project that included participants in Uganda and Kenya, as well as people in Alabama, Florida, Tennessee, Texas, and Washington in the United States.

For this year's edition, special thanks go out to Cindy Camp, a teacher in Robinswood Middle School in Orlando, Florida, who devoted a sizable portion of her time to compile, type, and verify several pages of poetry by her students. These pieces are included in this volume. As always, the tireless efforts of Philip Matogo brought the Kiguli poetry together for the project. He also has been hard at work developing and securing supporters. We also would like to acknowledge artist, D. L. Gardner, who donated her sketches to illustrate each chapter. Our cover design was the created by Matt Ostrom.

Special thanks go out to Major General James Mugira. He is Kiguli's literature club patron and Chairman of the School Management Committee, Kiguli Army Primary School, Nakasongola.

A final note from the publisher of this edition, Citron Concassé, LLC. It is our honor and our pleasure to help secure the future of this project and we hope that our contribution helps to keep the living heart of Kiguli poetry alive and well in the world.

Our family, friends, and those we choose to love…

Songs of Kiguli

Mother of my mother,
You gave birth to every beautiful daughter
Who later passed on that beauty to me.
You taught her to be very caring.
That is why she took very good care of me.
So proud of you mother of my mother.

Mother of my mother,
You were always there for her.
Whenever she fell down,
You would lift her up
And wipe her tears.
Whatever you did to her
She did to me.
So proud of you mother of my mother.

Mother of my mother,
Your love is like God's love.
You spent sleepless nights
Just to make sure she was comfortable.
No one else but you, would do that for her.
I thank God for your life.
May your soul rest in eternal peace.

By: Mahoro Jesca
Uganda

International Edition

Mother! Mother! Mother!
How important are you?
When I am away from home, I get worried of you,
You cook food for me when I am at school.
That's why I love you so much.

Mother! Mother! Mother!
When I am crying, you carry me.
When my dad is away, you work hard for money
To pay my school fees.
That's why I miss you so much.

Mother! Mother! Mother!
You are on the top of my heart.
If you are not there, I could easily die.
Because you are the one carrying my heart.
When you go away, I can easily burst.
That's why I love you.

By: Nasazi Diana
Uganda

Father! Father!
How important a person are you in my life!
You pay school fees for me.
You buy for me clothes to wear.

Father! Father!
You are an important person in the world.
Father without you I cannot have the food at home.
Father you are very useful.

By: Nakimuli Hawa
Uganda

Mother! Mother!
How useful are you?
You create fun for us.
You make us laugh.
You make us happy.

Mother! Mother!
And you care for us.
Without you I can be hungry.

Mother! Mother!
Without the family mother
We don't care for ourselves.
Mother how important are you?

By: Nakimuli Hawa
Uganda

In the Womb

In the womb of my mother
I was secure and peaceful.
The day I was born I cried
Because the maternity ward was closed.
I felt unhappy and peace was no more.
She knew I wanted breast milk and warmth.

In the womb of my mother
Nothing disturbed me and all was okay.
I would be peaceful and secure on earth.
But thieves and Killers worry by life.
Bomb blasts and child sacrifice scare me.
To hell with you who fight peace and security.
All Ugandans, let us plant peace for peace.

By: Otim Solomon
Uganda

Grandmother! Grandmother! Grandmother!
How important are you!
You tell us stories of long ago.
People of long ago were like dogs.

Grandmother! Grandmother! Grandmother!
You go to the garden to bring food.
And plant trees.
She tells stories when I'm with my friends.

By: Namugenyi Dorothy
Uganda

Child abuse! Child abuse!

You are bad.
Why do you torture us?
Don't you know we are young?
You damage our minds.
For how long will this be?

Child abuse! Child abuse!
For how long are we going to be neglected?
We are denied food and clothes.
Defilement and rape is a song everywhere.
Day and night, doing child labour.
For how long will this be?

Child abuse! Child abuse!
Away you must go.
Arise fellow Ugandans.
Fight child abuse.

By: Hipe Martha
Uganda

Grandfather! Grandfather! Grandfather!
Grandfather sits in a wheel chair.
He keeps watch over millet and sorghum.
He waves a stick or throws a stone
To scare the birds away from the courtyard

Grandfather! Grandfather! Grandfather!
Grandmother looks on from the verandah
As she weaves a colourful mat.
She cares for baby Sarah
Whose mother is away in the field.

Grandfather! Grandfather! Grandfather!
When aunt and uncle visit us
They will enjoy meat and rice with mother.

By: Namugenyi Dorothy
Uganda

Family! Family!
There's nothing as good as a family.
There's not a place as dear as family.
There I meet dad and mum.
There I share lots of fun.
With sister and bothers.
A bond together by blood.

Family! Family!
There's nothing as loving as a family.
There's not a place as caring as a family.
All members related to one another.
Uncles versus aunts as
Nephews compete with nieces.
And cousins beating them all.
All about love and care.

Family! Family!
There are stories of long ago,
As told by grandparents.
As interesting as the cultural tales.
The in laws have come.
Commanding due respect from
All Corners.
The family together we stay.
In it is as sweet as paradise.

By: Namulondo Sarah
Uganda

International Edition

REVENGE!

Revenge, disgusted
Getting back at my sister
GET OUT OF MY ROOM!

By: Shakeria Bright
Florida, USA

Jealousy Haiku

There was a couple
Who got married on the sea
Filled with jealousy

They wondered what life
Would be and society
Cute life on the sea

By: Chinilly Brice
Florida, USA

Hate

People like to hate
She is a fake best friend
I hate it so bad!

Hate hater's so bad
People will hate, be ready
Ready when they hate

By: Talanya Cunningham
Florida, USA

Found Poem

Happy Birthday!
January
Birthday Buddies
    friendship
feel special!
    extra special.

By Talanya Cunningham
Florida, USA

Friends

Friends are the best thing to have
But just make sure you don't get stabbed
And just adjust and grab on to yourself
Don't be afraid Don't go on a raid
Just come and stay - Don't leave us alone
Let's play on our phones
Let's go to the gas station
There is no equation.
There is no inflation, if we are not
friends. Don't stay till the end.

By: Emmanuel Garcia
Florida, USA

Found Poem

The
L-O-V-E. filled IN "My"
World Make LIFE
smiling friends and family, POWER
+ pride in THE World

By: Aniyah Hall
Florida, USA

My blessing poem

You are a perfect gift from God,
A blessing that everyone wants,
You are the most amazing thing to ever grace this earth.
When I look at you I see perfection, beauty in the eye of the beholder.
You give me the type of love that consumes me,
confidence that everybody needs.
I desire to give you this poem for you to understand how much you mean to me.
Our love will never die nor will our destiny
Even though we fight you're always there for me.

By: Aijha Keith
Florida, USA

Love What a Wonder

Love what a wonder
curious of the feeling
sunny or cloudy?

Feeling amazing
Or feeling the pain it caused
Don't know what to do.

By: Ashlyne Renelique
Florida, USA

How we stay healthy, get well, and how we die...

Stomach! Stomach! Stomach!
Mr. and Mrs. Stomach.
Who are you to make people suffer?
Because of you
You make people keep bags of money.
You make people to work for you.

Stomach! Stomach! Stomach!
You make people steal.
How bad you are?
You made Adam and Eve eat the forbidden fruit.
I wish you could die.
I may kill you.

By: Ajuma Benaleta
Uganda

Stomach, Stomach.
Mr. and Mrs. Stomach.
Who are you to make people suffer?
You make ministers and presidents go to work.

Oh Stomach!
You make priests beg for money to feed you.
Who are you that you cannot get food for yourself?

Oh Stomach!
You made Adam and Eve eat the forbidden fruit.
Now we are suffering because of you!

Oh Stomach!
What a dangerous thing you are.

By: Mukisa Remniy
Uganda

Every day
I need to eat fruits and vegetables
Rich in vitamins to fight diseases.
Mangoes, oranges, tomatoes and cabbages.
Grown at home and in school gardens.

Every day
I need to eat foods
Full of carbohydrates for energy and heart.
Cassava, potatoes, bananas and millet,
Grown at home and in school gardens.

Every day
I need to eat foods
Containing proteins to help me grow well.
Peas, beans, eggs, simsim and fish.
To complete my daily balanced diet.

Teacher says…
A body without soldiers
Falls sick more often.
A body lacking proteins
Remains stunted for life!

By: Kanyesigye Herbert
Uganda

Self-care! Self-care! Self-care!
When I am hungry
I get something to eat
To satisfy my hunger.
Because when I let the stomach go empty
I invite ulcers to myself.

Self-care! Self-care! Self-care!
When I feel thirsty
I think of something to drink
To satisfy my thirst.
Because when I let my throat go dry
I invite wounds.
Yes, water is life.

By: Kato Ivan
Uganda

HIV!! HIV!!
You are a bad disease.
You took my parents,
My mother and my father
Are dead.

HIV!! HIV!!
You are not good.
But I will keep myself.
You will not take me HIV!

By: Tusinakure Sylvia
Uganda

Aids! Aids!
Where did you come from?
Why did you come?
You are so deadly.
What a merciless destructor you are!

Young or old you destroy
None have escaped.
Doctors, the mechanics of life, have not been missed.
Teachers the doctors of ignorance, are also going.
Oh Aids! You are nonselective.

Merciless Aids!
You have left orphans helpless.
Widows have remained in suspense.
Easy to count citizens in a country
With mourning everywhere
When will you wish us bye?

By: Hipe Martha
Uganda

Diseases!
How strong you are.
Weakening the weak and the strong,
Disturbing the bodies of all.
Causing a lot of pain and sometimes death.

Diseases!
Typhoid, tuberculosis, cholera, and so on.
Who created you?
And from where did you come?
Why can't you leave us in peace?
When shall we get rid of you?

Diseases!
Hospitals, clinics,
All are filled to capacity,
What should be done to prevent diseases?
Sick people should be taken for treatment.
Infected people should be separated from the healthy.

By: Otim Solomon
Uganda

Aids! Aids! Aids!
You kill young and old.
We don't have a cure.
You killed my grandfather and grandmother.
Who brought you on earth to kill my grands?

Aids! Aids! Aids!
You are caused by a virus called
Human Immuno-deficiency virus (HIV).
You make a person feel tired
Though not as a result of physical activity.
You cause a person drastic loss of weight.

Aids! Aids! Aids!
Are you transmitted through body fluids?
You destroy a person's ability to fight off
Any infectious diseases.
You make a person become weak.
You make us to suffer.
To expose us to diseases that attack the brain,
Lungs, and nervous system.

By: Namulando Peace
Uganda

Death! Death! Death!
You are not fair.
Not fair at all.
Why are you not?
For God's sake!

Death! Death! Death!
Everybody fears you.
You are so much dreaded.
But not honoured.
Because you are fair.

Death! Death! Death!
One day, old ones.
Youthful, energetic, learned,
VIPS and intellectuals,
Save none but all swallowed!

Oh, Death! Death!
When will you get content?
Day and night you swallow!
Your belly never fills up.
Who are you, really, Death?

By: Namulando Peace
Uganda

First aid! First aid!
It all happened like a dream.
So swift and disturbing it was,
When I fell from a mango tree,
And broke my arm.

First aid! First aid!
It all happened like a dream.
Tumbling through the branches I fell,
Landing on the ground like a log.
But Mum had warned me never to climb trees.

First aid! First aid!
It all happened like a dream.
In such a disturbed mind I was,
Sitting straight and still in fear,
Wondering what my mother would say.

First aid! First aid!
It all happened like a dream.
Through disappointment,
Mother gave me first aid,
That reduced the pain.
And later took me to the hospital.

By: Akello Faith
Uganda

Doctor! Doctor! Doctor!
What an important person you are!
You save people's lives
By treating the sick.
Oh! Doctor, I wish I were you.

Doctor! Doctor! Doctor!
How important are you?
I wish I were you.
You treat also the president.
You treat any kind of disease.
I wish I were you.

Doctor! Doctor! Doctor!
How important are you?
You treat those who suffer from any disease.
Oh! Doctor! I wish I were you.

By: Akello Faith
Uganda

Sanitation! Sanitation!
If you don't practice sanitation
You will be attacked by diseases
Which will bring pain and death to people.

Sanitation! Sanitation!
If you don't practice sanitations
You will suffer from cholera, diarrhea, and malaria.

Sanitation! Sanitation!
If you want to prevent causing diseases
Practice the following activities.
Destroy stagnant water,
Slash around the compound.

By: Hatsemwa
Uganda

Mosquitoes! Mosquitoes! Mosquitoes!
You are not a friendly insect.
You and your wives frequently visit us.

Mosquitoes! Mosquitoes! Mosquitoes!
You have sharp tubes that suck our blood.
You have thin legs and small wings which
Prevent us from hearing you.
You carry malaria.

Mosquitoes! Mosquitoes! Mosquitoes!
I know what to do to prevent you.
I am going to drain your breeding places.
I will also slash away the bush around my house.
With that I will be able to stop you
From coming to my home.

By: Mubbala Elivis
Uganda

DEATH HAIKU

Opposite of life
Never know when it happens
It's coming for us

By: Rhain Powell
Florida, USA

WAR-PEACE Haiku

Messing with my gun
I shot him down where he stood
And then I felt bad

By Akelye Scurry
Florida, USA

DRUGS

Drain your brain Dull.
Ruin your life forever.
Unkind like a storm.
Gross
Strong as steel

By: Aniyah Hall
Florida, USA

Earth, wind, water, and fire…

Water! Water! Water!
You are very useful to us.
Without you we do not live.
You make people happy because of you.

Water! Water! Water!
How useful you are to people.
People use you for bathing.
People use you for washing their clothes.

Water! Water! Water!
You are useful to animals.
You make farmers' crops grow well.
Without you they can easily dry.

By: Letisha Maria
Uganda

Fire! Fire! Fire!
How important are you?
You provide light at night.
You make people warm.
What an important thing are you?

Fire! Fire! Fire!
How useful are you?
You are used in cooking food.
You are used in burning rubbish,
Which can make our compound dirty.

Fire! Fire! Fire!
How useful are you?
You are used in roasting meat and fish,
Which makes them dry up.
Then we sell the food to get money.

By: Nasazi Diana
Uganda

Water! Water! Water!
You give us life.
We use you to cook our food.
We use you in hospitals.
We use you to make juice.

Water! Water! Water!
We use you to wash our clothes.
We use you in generating hydro electrical power.
You give us water for animals.
We use you in bathing.
We use you in transport.

Water! Water! Water!
How useful you are to us.
We cannot live without you.
We thank God because he created you.
How useful water is!

By: Akankunda Justine
Uganda

International Edition

Wind! Wind!
Wind blows in different directions.
It blows to south, west, north east.
But still wind is good.
People feel good whenever wind blows.
Especially when the day is hot.
Wind reduces the hot temperature.

When the day is cold
People may not like the wind.
It makes them feel cold.
But all the same, wind is good.

Wind makes people scratch their heads.
Because they cannot see it.
They just feel it with their skins.
They, therefore, use different instruments.
To know its direction and speed
Oh wind is wonderful!

By: Ohangole Johnson
Uganda

Songs of Kiguli

Our climate, our seasons…

Rainbow! Rainbow! Rainbow!
Look up at the sky!
There is a round, semicircular object.

Look up at the sky!
What is that?
It's a rainbow.
How it is so nice to look at!
Look! It is beautiful.

Look! It is beautiful,
Oh yes it has shining colours.
What are the shining colours?
These are colours that are nice to look at.

By: Tosinaldire Sylvia
Uganda

Sun, oh the Sun!
The sun gives us sunlight.
It is the light of the world.
From its rays we find life.
How important the sun is!

The Sun makes the plants to grow.
It helps in photosynthesis.
Flowers bear fruits because of it.
How important the sun is!

The sun gives us vitamins.
It also gives us warmth.
We need it when we feel cold.
Thank you, god, for the sun!

By: Morris
Uganda

Sun!
When the sun comes the darkness goes away.
That means sun gives us light.
The light of the world.
From its rays we find life.
How important the sun is!

The sun makes the plants to grow.
Helps in photosynthesis.
The sun helps farmers to dry their crops.
Flowers bear fruit because of it.
How important the sun is!

The sun gives us vitamin D.
It also gives us warmth.
Thank you, God, for the sun.

By: Mukisa Renimy
Uganda

When the sky turns blue
Clouds run away fast.
And nature gets a clear view,
Of the king on his throne.
His Majesty, the Sun!

When His Majesty smiles,
There is rejoicing everywhere.
Birds, insects, plants, and animals
All sing, dance, and praise.
His Majesty, the Sun!

When His Majesty disappears
Darkness overpowers light.
And natures goes to sleep.
Except the strange few that remain awake,
To hunt for food at night.

Your Majesty, the Sun!
Our lives depend on you.
The soil marries your heat and rays
To make food for us to eat.
Long live Your Majesty, the Sun!

By: Kabazarwe Scovia
Uganda

Songs of Kiguli

Lightning! Lightning
Who are you?
You are a hag of war to us.
You are destroying our properties.
You are refusing us to stand under the trees.
You are merciless.

Lightning! Lightning!
Who are you?
You don't disappear under the rain.
When it is raining,
You are ever present.

Lightning! Lightning!
Who are you?
Why don't you leave us in peace?
You are dangerous.
You have a friend called thunder.

Lightning! Lightning!
Who are you?
You have a friend who scares people.
Some even reach the extent of collapsing.
Some people lose their lives because of your friend.
You should stop that because you are
finishing the world.

By: Kaguta Aron
Uganda

My Favorite Weather Is Rain

Rain is a peaceful moment to rest and
relax your body during the sweet sound
of water tapping on your window

By: Sabine Bocico
Florida, USA

A Frosty Hurricane

Flurries begin with a small wind gust
Mother nature just lost my trust
Extremity begins with a cold front
Snow falls in lust

This monsters time is now to confront
So same too begin the battlefront
For this devil in disguise
Who is on the hunt

Who has caused so many cries
Who has cost so many lives
Soon this curse will be lifted
This is sharper than knives

All the snow has drifted
If only we were all gifted
This beast has shifted
To other lands. But finally, this curse is lifted.

By: Michael Boodram
Florida, USA

Winter

Winter is my favorite time of the year, you know
I hate the blizzard, but I love the snow
Every time when winter is near
All the time, I always feel sincere

Winter for everyone is kind of a test
But winter for me is really the best
Winter for everyone they'll be in a daze
But winter for me, I'll be really amazed

By: Chinilly Brice
Florida, USA

Global warming is a serious conflict, but not many people realize that. One day we are going to wake up and find all animals and plants dead and lava spewing out everywhere because of our reckless technology usage.

By: Widjina Jean-Giles
Florida, USA

Winter

The coldest season of them all
It's the season where the snow falls

The coldest season has my favorite holiday
When kids get new toys and like to play

You will need a lot of layers of clothes
A lot of socks with your shoes to cover up your toes

Going outside to make a snowman.
The snow is cold so I put gloves on my hands.

Winter is my favorite season of all
I like winter better than Summer, Spring, and Fall

In Mississippi, on a cold winter day
The sun comes out and makes the snow go away

You might get sick with a stopped up nose.
Can't breathe well because your nostrils seemed closed

IN winter time cut off your fans.
Turn on your heat and warm your hands

By: Gavin Brinker
Florida, USA

Fall

The autumn comes for all
As the leaves fall,
you can say that it's better than them all.
Nature is telling the trees to start over
like the very beautiful 4-leaf clover.
Family comes from far and near
to celebrate Thanksgiving that is almost here.
It's better than it appears as fall is nearly here.
As the wind is blowing
No time for snowing
No grass needs mowing
It's nice knowing
About the weather that is coming, where it's not cold and not sunny
And it's kinda funny
Because the power that is instilled with me
To make this rhyming trilogy
It's kinda plain to see, the season that is made for me.

By: Gerald Castor
Florida, USA

Summer

We plan to go in pools
That always seem to be cool
The 4th of July
We all turn to fools

It's always a sign
That it's time to say, "Hi."
It's almost my birthday
And we should be ready to then say goodbye.

And for that I'm certain
But it's usually a burden
I don't like the heat
We had to pull down the curtains

I feel like I'll go crazy
I would love it if it felt a little breezy
It would be better if it was freezing
That would be amazing

By: Ruthnie Denais
Florida, USA

Winter

Playing in the snow
With our Christmas bows
A happy break from school
Temperatures always low
Feeling really cool
Even if we can't go in the pool
Listening to music
While working with our tools
Wearing my tunic
Spending time with family
Who are a bunch of lunatics
Living life happily
Building things craftily
While my cousin, Cassity
is sleeping lazily

By: Daniela Gonzalez
Florida, USA

Spring

Spring is cool
The time I act like a fool
Let's go to the pool
It is the weekend, I don't have to go to school
I don't want to take a test
I just want to watch Johnny Test
And my room is a mess
It's that start of a new life
Flowers do not bloom at night
The next morning I flew my kite
This is the time of my birthday
Can I get a snake?
Then maybe a cake?
Eat a bunch of steak!
A new invention it is time to make
I hope it doesn't break.

By: Jason Hannah
Florida, USA

Snow

Racing down a snow covered hill
As fast as a rocket, such a thrill
With snow falling down on our hair and clothes
All you want to do is stop for a moment, stick your tongue out and stand still
As you come to a stop at the bottom of the hill, you feel something chilly on your nose
You try to see what is that thing, and you stare in awe as it gleams and glows
So small, so beautiful, so white, and so magically special
There is no two alike, as far as anybody knows
When they fall from the sky, it really takes you to a whole new level
And now they're all over you, they're several.

By: Widjina Jean Giles
Florida, USA

Spring Morning was Near is Here

Birds singing so brightly in the mornings
Everything around me is so lively, nothing is boring
Spring is in the air
And gerbils waking up from their snoring

Colors are everywhere
The winter is gone, but the memory is still there
Sunny skies and silly lies
Everything seems to be jumping like the rabbit hare

Time really just flies
When you're eating Easter pies
Flowers come and grow
And birds fly in the skies

What an amazing show
It just glows
like snow
but no.

By: Stephanie Joseph
Florida, USA

Autumn

Autumn is the best season!!!
and there is way more than 1 reason
first of all it's cool
also it barely freezin'

Another world for autumn is fall
the trees are colorful and tall
the trees are kinda going bald
this season has people bouncin' off the wall

Already time to eat, I'm ready to dive-in
But first "knock knock" the family is just arrivin'
Sprint to the door, then we get ready to eat Thanksgivin'
Now it's time to start huggin'

"Brrr" we're getting close to wintertime to wear long sleeves
Just made a pile, time to jump in the leaves
Mom and dad it's my birthday buy me a present oh please
Because getting nothing for my birthday is a real pet peeve

By: Julien Montilus
Florida, USA

Spring

When it comes to Spring,
Goodbye to skating rinks.
It's time to sing
and the church bells ring!

Here is a season
to commit no treason.
There are many reasons,
To not be freezin'

There is a world full of snow
But there is still hope.

Seasons

All four seasons come and go
Within all four seasons you should try to grow

By: Kadeem Simmonds
Florida, USA

Summer

It's time for life to get funner
No school is no bummer
All of the fun and laughter outside
I don't need a sweater

Going for a boat ride
or to the park to see the birds glide
Run then leap into the pool
When it's over we all want to cry

The water is super cool
time for me to be a fool
I had such a great day

Could not spend it any other way
Tomorrow is another day to play
Can build my day up like clay
All that can be said for summer is yay!

By: Rhain Powell
Florida, USA

R-ough days at school and work
A-reas filled with water like ponds and rivers
I-ndoors all day long
N-ever ending rain singing songs

By: Aijha Keith
Florida, USA

Winter

Playing in the winter snow
is all I know
making snow angels and snowmen
can be quite a show

now and then
you can see children
snuggled up by the fire
while parents laugh and talk in the den

having fun in the cold, snowy weather can be such a tire
but the need for a warm drink and a meal for the homeless is
dire
getting ready to fall asleep
they dream of getting higher

counting the many sheep
God will help me through this leap
they say to themselves in their thoughts so deep
but winter memories are something I want to keep

By: Alyra Washington
Florida, USA

Spring

When it comes to Spring,
Goodbye to skating rinks.
It's time to sing
and the church bells ring!

Here is a season
to commit no treason.
There are many reasons,
To not be freezin'

There is a world full of snow
But there is still hope.

By Natalie Santisteban
Florida, USA

Seasons

All four seasons come and go
Within all four seasons you should try to grow
You should try to grow as a person

And if you don't grow instantly just keep workin'

Just keep workin' towards your goals
Like the little mustard seed, it grows and grows

It grows and grows towards the sun
Until Fall comes when it's growing is done

It's growing is done throughout the winter
It's growing is done, 'til on come the sprinklers

The sprinklers come on, during the spring
During spring, our flowers quietly sing

They quietly sing, towards a tune
Towards the tune, while they slowly bloom.

By: Kadeem Simmonds
Florida, USA

Songs of Kiguli

Cars, and trains, and planes…

Songs of Kiguli

Travelling is a good thing
Whether by water,
By road, or by air.
There is a lot to see.
Gardens, and plantations,
Hills, and lakes.

Passengers from all over the country,
With or without luggage.
Pupils on their way to school.
Patients on their way to clinics.
Tourists on their way to the National Game Parks,
And holiday makers of all races.

By: Naturinda Daphine
Uganda

Travelling! Travelling! Travelling!
Travelling is a good thing whether by water,
By road, or by air, there is plenty to see.
Gardens and plantations.
Islands and animals.

Travelling! Travelling! Travelling!
Passengers from all over the world,
With or without luggage.
Pupils on their way to school.
Patients on their way to clinics.
Tourists on their way to zoos.
And holiday makers of all races.

Travelling! Travelling! Travelling!
Travelling by train is fun -
As the engine pulls a long "snake."
Getting faster down the valley,
As passengers see the beautiful landscape,
As they share experiences,
With the different people they meet.

By: Kato Ivan
Uganda

Travelling! Travelling! Travelling!
Whether by water, or road, or air.
There is plenty to see.
Gardens and plantations.

Travelling! Travelling! Travelling!
Passengers from all continents.
Doctors on their way to hospitals.
Teachers on their way to school.

Travelling! Travelling! Travelling!
Travelling by train is amazing.
As the engine pulls a long "snake."
As passengers see the beautiful landscape.
With different people they meet.

By: Namugenyi Dorothy
Uganda

Roads! Roads!
How important you are,
You help us to travel to different places.

Roads! Roads!
Without you there is no movement,
Of people from one place to another.
You lead us to our place of work.
You are sometimes straight in shape.

By: Makubuya Rashid
Uganda

Road accidents.
Robbers of human life.
Blood splashing the roads.
What a carnage.

Road accidents.
Snatchers of human souls.
Pieces of flesh scattered on the road.
What a waste!

Road accidents.
Agents of human depopulation.
Corpses entangled in wrecked vehicles on roads.
What a tragedy!

By: Ogwane Moses, Namulondo Peace
Uganda

Conductor
This is my bus fare.
Give me a ticket quickly.
I want to go to Kampala,
To lead a better life.

Conductor
This is my first trip
Far away from home.
When we reach the city,
Direct me to Old Taxi Park.

Neighbour
I'm tired of rural life,
Where life is wasted in gardens.
Toiling and sweating in rain and hot sun
To grow food to eat!

Driver! Driver!
Step on the gas please.
I want to reach the city quickly,
And look for opportunities,
To lead a better life!

By: Morris, Alado Bonica Teddy
Uganda

Toyota Harrier!
You are a model car.
So fast running you are.
I trust your speed when going up country.
My Harrier, you have never let me down.

You are a comfortable car.
A car I enjoy sitting in and driving around.
Your air conditioner is good.
You are a nice-looking car.
You are a car of the millennium.

When others talk about Ipsum,
I talk about a Toyota Harrier.
For it makes my life easier and comfortable.
I don't regret that I bought it.

You are trusted and secure.
You cause few accidents.
Second to you is a Hummer.
Though it is slightly more expensive.
You serve and have the same function.

By: Mutoni Queen, Namugenyi, Dorothy
Uganda

Songs of Kiguli

Best Built African Car
It is a front-wheel drive station wagon,
With optional seating up to eight.
A wagon that is a delight,
Rather than a chore, to drive.

Best Built African Car
A wagon where design,
And engineering come,
Together in one functional unit.
Its shape even used the wind
To help turns press its tires on
The pavement for road gripping.

Best Built African Car
As Ford Quality Job One.
A 1985 survey established,
Ford makes the Best Built African Car.
It is based on an average of problems
Reported by the owners,
During six months on '81-'84 models
Designed and built in Africa.

By: Musasizi Mike
Uganda

The things we grow and raise, the things we eat...

Songs of Kiguli

Flowers! Flowers!
Everywhere I turn
My eyes light up.
Beautiful colours everywhere.
What an opportunity this is for me!

Flowers! Flowers!
Roses, daises, orchids and all.
Red, yellow and purple flowers.
Decorating homes, schools and offices.
Filling the air with pleasant scents!

Flowers! Flowers!
Busy bees in love with them.
Buzzing from one to the other
Collecting nectar for honey
That you and I love to eat!

Flowers! Flowers!
A flower farm I'll make
And place bee hives in it.
I'll make money from flowers,
And chase poverty away

By: Namulondo Peace
Uganda

Oh my little flower,
How lovely you look!
I put you on the dining table,
And you looked to nice.
I the put you beside the TV
And you looked so great.
I decided to put you beside my bed
And everybody admired you.

But now my little flower
You are becoming small each day.
You are dying away too fast
When I still want to see you.
What should I do
To make you stay longer?
I think I should put you
In a tin of water.

By: Noyamuhai Elizabeth
Uganda

Songs of Kiguli

Sweet Potatoes! Sweet Potatoes!
How sweet you are!
Everybody likes you because you are sweet.

Sweet Potatoes! Sweet Potatoes!
You make my stomach big.
Without you I cannot live.

By: Makubuya Rashid
Uganda

Farm! Farm! Farm!
From the farm
Is where I get all this happiness.
All this strength and income0
For there lives a friend,
A friend so generous.

Milk you give me,
When my mother is at work.
Manure you give the plantation.
The plantation that later gives me matooke,
To survive the hunger,
When my mother is away.

So generous, you give skin too.
To make the drums to entertain me
When I feel bored and tired.
But I don't give, all this you give me.
But I don't give anything back,
Not even shelter.
What kind of creature am I?

By: Alado Bonica Teddy
Uganda

Which is more useful?
I help plants grow well!
Cries the loam soil.
For I am full of fertilizers
Which help in the growing of plants.

I help man build houses!
Cries the sand soil.
When I am mixed with cement
I make strong buildings.

I am useful to some wild animals!
Cries the clay soil.
I also help man get
Raw materials like clay and papyrus,
To make the pots and baskets,
Which he later sells for money.

By: Tayebwa Keneth
Uganda

Animals! Animals! Animals!
You are very useful to us.
You are source of income.
You are so sweet.
People eat you on Christmas and Easter.

Animals! Animals! Animals!
You make people happy because of you.
But the disadvantage of you.
Is that you make people's compound dirty.

Animals! Animals! Animals!
How important you are.
People keep you because you are useful.
You make farmers' crops grow well
By giving them manure.

By: Maria Letisha
Uganda

Songs of Kiguli

Animals, funny creatures.
They don't talk but communicate.
But different sounds they make
Enable them to communicate,
Any time they want.

Animals, funny creatures.
They do not work nor dig,
But can't wait to feed.
They are cared for
By man and the Almighty Lord,
Every time they want, and to their satisfaction.

Animals, funny creatures.
Loved by people
For people get many good things from them.
Milk and meat for food,
Skins for decoration and clothes,
Dung for farm manure.

Animals, funny creatures.
Can cause harm if offended.
With bites, kicks, hitting, scratching.
And, oh! Can cause death.
Take care whenever you deal with animals.

By: Otim Solomon
Uganda

Animals are useful.
They carry people all day
To different places.
Mostly in desert areas
Like Sahara and Namibi deserts.

Animals are useful.
Their waste is manure.
There are other things,
Like cultural purposes,
Meat, and mohair production.

Plants are also useful.
They're used as wind breakers.
They reduce soil erosion.
They are food like
Root crops, and fruits.
Some leaves are sauce,
Like dodo leaves.

By: Morris
Uganda

Bees! Bees!
Bees are very dangerous to people.
Bees are bad insects.
When you disturb them
They become dangerous to you.
Bees protect themselves by stinging.

Bees! Bees!
Bees are important in the following ways.
Bees provide us with honey.
Bees provide is with wax.

Bees! Bees!
You are dangerous to people.
In many ways.
Stinging people who come to collect honey.
You sting people in order to protect yourselves.

By: Mubbala Elivis
Uganda

International Edition

Cock Robin! Cock Robin! Cock Robin!
Who killed Cock Robin?
"I." Said the crow.
"With my bow and arrow.
I killed Cock Robin."

Cock Robin! Cock Robin! Cock Robin!
Who caught his blood?
"I" Said the cat.
"With my small dish
I caught his blood."

Cock Robin! Cock Robin! Cock Robin!
Who saw him dying?
"I." Said the rat.
"With my little eyes,
I saw him dying."

By: Namugewyl Dorothy, Makubuya Rashid,
Namajja Irene, Ndyamuhaki Elizabeth
Uganda

American Food Haiku

Chick-fil-a nuggets
fries. Delicious every time
Best cow in whole world!

By: Aijha Keith
Florida, USA

Food

Is delicious to me
It is all around people
Everyone eats it

By: Brad Sinanan
Florida, USA

How we learn, how we build knowledge…

If I didn't have ten fingers
I couldn't count to ten.
I always use my fingers
They are better than my pens.

If I didn't have ten fingers
I couldn't even add
Without my trusty fingers
My math is really sad!

I use these handy fingers for math.
Do no ask me why.
I use these handy fingers
Like stars light up the sky!
But now my teacher is says – no!

Do it in my head.
If fingers are forbidden
I will use my toes instead!

By: Nankynola Hope
Uganda

Education! Education!
You give us knowledge,
To become good workers.
If you are not there,
We live a peace-less life.

Education! Education!
Young and old need you
To learn good things.
We need you and your presence
In order to enjoy good life.

Education! Education!
Although you can't be seen,
We should make you useful.
People have got good jobs
Because of you.
You are the key.
The key to everything on earth.

By: Hipe Martha
Uganda

Education!

Education is important in the world.
Oh, education!
You make us to be skillful.
You make us to acquire knowledge.
You make us know more about the world.

People are educated in many ways.
Education! You are so good to us.
You help make plans of our future,
In order to help us become good citizens.

By: Mukisa Remmy
Uganda

Education, the key to success!
You are so good to us.
You make people live successfully.
If one doesn't get you,
One will have a difficult future.

Education, the key to success!
People are happy because of you.
People are willing to have you.
People have learned how to read and write.

Education, the key to success!
People have discovered many good things.
Things like computers and phones.
Oh! Education! How good you are!

By: Mubbala Elivis
Uganda

Songs of Kiguli

School Child! School Child!
How hard your school days are!
Rain or shine, nobody cares
To do chores first.

School Child! School Child!
How hard your school days are!
To school you run bare footed.
Stones cut into your feet,
To reach school before classes begin.

School Child! School Child!
How hard you school days are!
Hunger is your daily companion.
Your nose becomes your mouth.

School Child! School Child!
How hard school days are!
Not a single moment for you to relax.
Do this and to that fills the air.
At school and at home.
When shall I leave school?

By: Kagaga Winnie
Uganda

P.L.E. P.L.E. P.L.E.
We are ready to face it.
All the teachers have been preparing us for it.
They say they need aggregate four.
It is made of up four main subjects.
P.L.E. is the scoring word.

Some are made to repeat a class.
All because they didn't pay attention,
To what P.L.E. requires of them.
I am one of those ready to face it.
Frightened always by the outcomes.
If negative, I am made to repeat,
If positive, I am promoted to S1.

Others just keep home during exam time.
They have not prepared well enough.
The timetable release makes them panic.
The best advice is to follow
The teachers' instructions.
They are the makers of the scoring -
Element, P.L.E.

By: Nansereko Aisha
Uganda

Teacher! Teacher!
What a great person you are!
You are patient and kind.
A mother away from home.
Wiping away my tears when I cry.

Teacher! Teacher!
What a great person you are!
Your heart is warm.
You listen to all my complaints,
Even when they are childish.

Teacher! Teacher!
What a great person you are!
You teach us games.
You give us knowledge.
Oh, Teacher! You are my greatest companion.

By: Baaty Gloria
Uganda

Exams! Exams!
The day has come.
The children run up and down
Fearing because they are not ready.
They were busy playing.

Exams! Exams!
May I go for a short call, teacher?
And refuse to come back,
But hide in the toilet,
Because things are hard.

Exams! Exams!
Questions are not easy
Oh! The poor marks I shall get!
Oh! God help me, they cry.
That I may go to S1.

By: Ndyamuhaki Elizabeth, Ogwane Moses
Uganda

Songs of Kiguli

The time is now!
The time-table is already fixed.
Come rain or shine,
There is no turning back now,
It's time to engage the monster!

The time in now
The time-table dictates
English and science today.
Maths and social studies tomorrow.
As decreed by UNEB for P.L.E.

The time is now!
The time-table is beckoning me,
To line up to be checked,
Before I enter the torture chamber,
To battle the monster with pen, pencil, and ruler.

The time is now!
The time-table is daring me,
To open the English language paper.
White as snow it leers at me.
And now the battle of brains must commence!

By: Nasasira Margret
Uganda

When will I be free?
As free as a bird in the air?
Caged in the classrooms no more,
And not given orders any more.

When will I be free?
To decide what to do?
To do my work and then play a game,
To watch TV and then have a rest.

When will I be free?
From all the tight rules around me?
And threats and sticks,
That make me weaker and weaker.

If there's any fee
To pay so as to be free,
Here I make my request,
That you inform me about it.

By: Nasasira Margret
Uganda

Newspapers Newspapers
Hey Mr. Newspaper Vender,
Can I take a look before I pay?
It's the cartoon page I like most,
For I laugh and laugh for the whole day.

Newspapers Newspapers
Do I read for pleasure?
Or just to reduce pressure?
And I read them for treasure!
Oh! Newspapers you make me happy.

The journalists, and the editors,
The columnists, and reporters,
The cartoonists, and photojournalists,
The whole staff always assists,
To make newspapers interesting.

By: Tayebwa Keneth
Uganda

International Edition

Newspapers! Newspapers!
What a great source of information and daily update
Of things happening around the world.
They contain various articles
On education, government, sports, and so on.

Newspapers! Newspapers!
New Vision, Daily Monitor or the Red Pepper
All compete to give information.
Be it right or wrong.
Vendors travel long distances from the source,
Looking for customers to buy them.
Indeed they end up successfully.

Newspapers! Newspapers!
Wait a minute!
Are those the only sources of information to us?
No! Not quite!
Computers, radio, and television,
Give more information to the public.
Thanks to all these sources.
How ignorant we would be without them!

By: Akankunda Justine
Uganda

Newspapers Newspapers
How important you are!
You give us news and information
About many things in the world.
Without you there is ignorance.

Newspapers Newspapers
How important you are.
You are a source of knowledge
To candidates all over Uganda.
Weekly exams and answers,
Without you there is failure.

Newspapers Newspapers
How expensive you are!
You are available to chosen few,
Who can afford to buy you to see,
Knowledge happiness and success.

By: Ogwane Moses
Uganda

Letters! Letters!
You are very useful to everybody.
All of us use you to air out our views.
We get a lot to learn after reading you.

Letters! Letters!
People write letters to say "Hello."
While others write letters to you,
As an invitation to birthday parties.

Letters! Letters!
To say sorry to the ones you've hurt --
Your request for permission to be away --
We seek advice from friends and relatives.
Indeed letters simplify our lives.

By: Namulondo Sarah
Uganda

Books! Books! Books!
Books everywhere for everyone.
Books at all times in full use.
Needed by all those with flesh.
The young and the old.
Running up and down as they open
In search for meaning of spelling,
From no source other than dictionaries,
As the best source.

Books! Books! Books!
Appearing in small and big volumes.
Fully packed with nothing but definitions.
Readers seriously enjoying the sweet arrangement.
Scanning and screaming through the pages
Of dictionaries and thesauruses,
Adding spelling power for writing.
Polishing pronunciation and of fluency spoken.
From no source other than a dictionary,
As the best source of vocabulary.

Books! Books! Books!
Not only does dictionary explain,
Giving meaning or spelling.
But also thesaurus does give
Arranged words according to families.
Groups of words with similar meanings.
Appearing in class groupings.
All but simplifying the work of mine,
From no source other than thesaurus,
As the best source of word families.

Books! Books! Books!
The most important non-living thing I know.
From you I can get all the knowledge I want.
With you I can become whatever I want to be.
A doctor, a teacher, an engineer, or a lawyer.
You are really wonderful!

Books! Books! Books!
We must find you in nursery school,
Primary, secondary, college, and even university.
The young and old are all looking for you to read.

Books! Books! Books!
The more books you read,
The better life you get.
For the young boys and girls,
I advise you to read more books,
If you want to have a bright future.

By: Kabazarwe Scovia
Uganda

Books! Books! Books!
The most important thing I know.
From you I can get all the knowledge I want.
With you I can be whatever I want to be,
A doctor, a teacher, a carpenter.
You are really wonderful.

Books! Books! Books!
We must find you in nursery school,
Primary, secondary, college and even university.
The young and old are all looking for you to read.

Books! Books! Books!
For the young boys and girls
I advise you to read more books
If you want to have a bright future.

By: Otim Solomon
Uganda

Letters! Letters!
You are very useful to everybody.
All of us use you to air out our views.
We get a lot to learn after reading you.

Letters! Letters!
People write letters to friends to say "Hello."
While others write invitations to Birthday parties.
You open up doors for others looking for jobs.

Letters! Letters!
To say sorry to the ones you've hurt,
You request permission to be away.
We seek advice from friends and relatives
Indeed letters simplify our lives.

By: Mubbala Elivis
Uganda

Letters! Letters!
You are friendly to everybody.
For you offer communication services to all.
Whether good or bad, you,
Still take them to their destinations.

You are a tool for expression,
So you need a reward.
For you are helpful to the youth and elderly,
Carrying messages of fun, irritation and business.
You've made communication easy.

But, my dear friend,
You still have a challenge to look at.
And that is a fellow competitor,
Which is the internet system.
That is efficient when it delivers.
You are in trouble, you should work hard.

By: Nanajja Irene
Uganda

Knowledge

Knowledge is key
To have success need knowledge
Knowledge is power

By: Jason Hannah
Florida, USA

School

Happiness at school
Hanging out at RMS
No stress
Have my favorite teachers
All day they're the best
Probably at the time right now I'm taking one of the hardest tests
I'll pass it like a basketball no contest
No time to tell you the rest
But I'll wish you the best.

By: Julien Montilus
Florida, USA

Songs of Kiguli

I go to a school, every day, to school I go
I go to a school where when you
first open and walk through the gate,
you can already see, hear and feel the hate.
I go to a school where when you first enter, you can already see
the students glare and whisper.
I go to school, every day, to school I go.

I go to a school where all that matters is if
my shoulders are showing
or if my dress is too short.
They say I can't wear my own skin
or else the boys won't pay attention
Why is what I wear more important than my own education?
I go to school, every day, to school I go.

I go to a school where if you're black and speak properly
they claim you are acting white.
But if you're white and sound ghetto,
they claim you're acting right.
I go to a school where acting white is treated as a sin
Because apparently, acting black is what's "in."
And that confuses me because it wasn't like that back then.

I can't believe that every morning,
everyday my mom tells me "go to school, it's good for you!
The teachers are nice and you'll make a lot of friends too."
Because every morning, every day, I go to a school where
I can be anyone but myself
because clearly the only opinion that matters
is the opinion of everyone else.

By: Yasmine Octelus
Florida, USA

Songs of Kiguli

How we communicate, our technology…

Communication! Communication!
An era when communication is so fast.
A generation where information is found everywhere.
A time when people don't go to classrooms to attend lessons.
A time when people transact business from their bedrooms,
But attend them through the internet.

Communication! Communication!
No more writing letters,
Because emails are faster.
No more writing applications,
Because fill in forms are easier.
No more selling goods door to door,
For customers are nearer on the internet.
Above all, a source of quick information.

Communication! Communication!
Every side you turn users waiting
For Internet café's to open.
Those with computers are busy surfing.
Telephone networks sending the internet to our phones.
What would this world be without the internet?

By: Ndyamuhaki Elizebeth
Uganda

Telephones! Telephones!
Whether fixed or mobile,
You do the same job,
As you connect people all the time.

Telephones! Telephones!
You work without rest.
You don't show that you are tired,
You just continue sending and receiving messages,
Containing sad and good news.

Telephones! Telephones!
Where did you get that knowledge,
Of calculating numbers of all types?
How did you get the wisdom,
About telling time and the date?

Telephones! Telephones!
You are a friendly partner.
You play the most enjoyable music,
You keep people's memory steady
With the pictures you take and store.

Uganda

Technology

The Revolution is HERE
CD is audio
DVD is video
So stop struggling with the VCR

By: Michael Boodram
Florida, USA

Our cultures, our country, and our society...

Who are you?
Ever and always alert,
To see any speeding vehicle and motorcycle.
Always guarding us.
Helping to maintain law and order.

Who are you?
Patrolling the road,
Always attending to accidents.
Always stationed on the road,
Helping us cross busy roads at the zebra crossing.

Who are you?
Arresting poor road users.
Stopping cases of mob riots.
Working like traffic lights.
To guide and control motorists and cyclists.

Oh, Oh! Traffic officers!
When I grow up I want to be like you,
Because I like to investigate crimes
Before arresting anyone.

By: Baaty Gloria
Uganda

Soldier! Soldier!
Tall and slim.
Always marching in the woods,
Tap, tap, go the boots.

Soldier! Soldier!
Plump and strong.
Always clad in green and black.
Left right go the steps

Soldier! Soldier!
War is raging.
Where do we go and hide ourselves?
Boom, boom go the bombs.

Soldier! Soldier!
Try your best,
To save our lives and save our property.
Let the rebels find it hard,
To stop the government of people.

By: Mboozi Joan
Uganda

Mr. Jailer –
Stop calling me a prisoner.
You rob me of my property,
Claiming to be a helper,
You are a hypocrite.

Mr. Jailer—
Stop calling me a prisoner.
Even when I die in prison,
You won't benefit.
Because you will die too.
You are a devil.

Mr. Jailer—
Stop calling me a prisoner.
You bribe the judges to hide,
The truth from my people,
So that I rot in cells.
You are really a monster.
Only God is the final judge.

By: Baaty Gloria
Uganda

What the police do!
The police are always alert.
Patrolling day and night,
Come rain and come sunshine.
The police are always on guard,
To maintain law and order.

What the police do!
The police are always on.
Patrolling the roads
Attending to accidents.
Stationed near the market.
Positioned at the stadium.
Saluting dignitaries
At the state house.

What the police do!
The difficult time
Is when statements are made and fines paid.
The witness wants the thief arrested.
But the police says wait,
We first investigate before arresting.
It is not a single job, my friend

By: Kawwine Grace
Uganda

Songs of Kiguli

The thieves!
Inside olden broken houses,
Sit and hide the evil men.
These are the dreaded thieves.
And they are always hungry.

The thieves!
In half-finished houses,
They wait and watch for nightfall,
To break into our houses and steal our property.
For they are always hungry.

The thieves!
Through brightest days and darkest nights,
These terrifyingly ugly people,
Await to beat and kill their victims.
For they are always hungry.

The thieves!
Warning! Watch out!
When you see any one you suspect,
Report fast to a nearby police station.
Because it might be you as the next victim.

By: Kamwine Grace
Uganda

I am a vendor.
A vendor am I.
On foot I travel everywhere,
Along streets and village paths,
Selling my goods to the young and old.

I am a vendor.
A vendor am I.
I carry all my goods.
Toys, cutlery, combs, and earrings.
On my head, arms and shoulders.

I am a vendor.
A vendor am I.
Whether hot or cold weather,
I sing as I walk,
To attract customers to buy.

I am a vendor.
A vendor am I.
Happy and full of joy at times,
When my pocket is heavy with coins and notes,
To feed me and pay fees.

By: Tayebwa Keneth
Uganda

Songs of Kiguli

Village woman! Village woman!
Look at the woman.
Tired hungry baby,
Clinging to her back.
And she herself so tired,
She drags her legs.
The firewood bundled on her head,
Weighs heavily.
But still she drags on.

Village woman! Village woman!
Her skin once smooth and lovely,
Is now wrinkled and dark.
Her cloths dirty and torn.
Her feet dirty and cracked.
When she reaches home,
Fetches water from the well,
Lights a fire, prepares the food.
There is more work in the field,
Until the sun sets.

Oh lord, when will she rest?

By: Naturnida Daphine
Uganda

Tourism! Tourism!
Tourism is great and important.
Tourists have improved on people lives.
They have created employment for some people.
Why some people are illiterates in the village and town!

Some people in town and village can
Get employed and the get money.
Tourists came to see an interesting thing,
And they paid money for it.
Then the employers get the money!

And mountain and game park
Attract tourists who bring income.
They promote beauty of environment
And beauty of a country like Uganda.
Uganda was developed by tourist attraction.
Uganda is a tourist attraction.

By: Mandilu James
Uganda

Songs of Kiguli

Hotels Hotels Hotels Hotels
In villages, towns, and cities.
All with one aim,
To remedy people's hunger and thirst
With food and drink.

Hotels Hotels Hotels Hotels
All with smartly dressed waitresses
And gentle welcoming waiters.
Who attend to the customers,
According to their wishful order,
As they ask for various kinds of food.

Hotels Hotels Hotels Hotels
With well varnished furniture and tidy toilets.
Some with saunas, gyms, and showers,
To make the customers feel at home,
As they spend their wonderful time there.

Hotels Hotels Hotels Hotels
Visit any like Africana or Serena.
You will wish you could stay there.
For the rest of your life.

By: Alado Bonica Teddy
Uganda

Money! Money!
Where is money for me?
To buy goods for my family,
Uniforms and fees for my children,
And pay doctors for treatment.

Money! Money!
I hunt for you everywhere.
Odd jobs are my daily meals.
In the hot sun and heavy rain.
Never a moment to rest.

Money! Money!
Sleepless nights are my companions.
Planning to trap and hold you.
But slippery as an eel you are.
For those without any education.

Money! Money!
Ruler of this world.
You have condemned us the poor
To die shamefully on
hunger –
diseases –

By: Nyangoma Shirah
Uganda

Culture! Culture!
This is a way we live,
Where information is passed
From eldest to the young,
To teach us how to behave.

Culture! Culture!
Each is proud of one's culture.
Naming, eating, speaking, dancing,
And important ceremonies,
Like introductions, weddings, etc.

Culture! Culture!
We should not despise our culture.
Because without it
We shall not kneel while greeting,
And no values will be promoted in our society.

By: Kagaga Winnie
Uganda

Rise up children!
There are many fights for rights.
Even among children on the streets,
Who are neglected and rejected,
Depressed and distressed,
Misused and abused.

These children on the streets,
Dressed in rags,
Addicted to drugs,
Wandering like stray dogs,
Disowned by their master.

There are children in homes,
Whose rights are but sad stories.
Whose stories are never told.
Whose voices are never heard.
Whose songs are never sung.

There are children in this country,
Whose rights are highly respected,
Whose life is meaningful.
They rise up to defend their rights.
They demand education, food, and care.
Rise up, children, fight for your rights!

By: Mandilu James
Uganda

Songs of Kiguli

Election! Election!
A period to canvass for votes.
Aspiring candidates vie for nominations,
And elected to different posts.

Election! Election!
Candidates launch their manifestos,
In rallies they promise,
What they will do for the voters.

Election! Election!
Local council elections,
Parliamentary and presidential elections.
Candidates move here and there campaigning.

Election! Election!
Voters throng to polling stations,
Voting for whom they want to lead them.
Then the winner takes it all.

By: Ohangole Johnson
Uganda

Uganda! Uganda! Uganda!
Oh, Uganda, our motherland.
You're called motherland
Because you are the heart of the world.
You are a land of milk and honey.
You are the paradise of the world.
You are ever green.

Uganda! Uganda! Uganda!
Oh, Uganda. The pearl of Africa.
Full of intelligent black people.
Look at the doctors, and teachers,
Engineers, and nurses, all born in Uganda.
The land of bright sunlight and physical beauty.

By: Ajuma Benaleta
Uganda

Physical features!
Physical features include
Lakes, rivers, mountains and hills.

Physical features!
How important you are.
You provide us with food.

Physical features!
You attract tourists.
You act as home for wild animals.

Physical features!
You provide charcoal to us.
You provide herbal medicine.

By: Klatsernwa Merabu
Uganda

I am a Ugandan and
Uganda is my homeland.
The pearl of Africa
Where rain and sunshine fuse
To make her abundantly fertile.

I am a Ugandan and
Uganda is my homeland.
With mountains and rolling plains.
Habitat to beautiful flora and fauna.
A heavenly destination for every tourist.

I am a Ugandan and
Uganda is my homeland.
The source of the legendary Nile,
Irrigating large fields of corn and rice.
A life blood to Egyptian and Sudanese and Egypt's youth.

I am a Ugandan and
Uganda is my homeland.
Black and proud I am.
United by strong bonds of cultural diversity.
Living in peace and harmony with one and all.

By: Lapyem Samuel
Uganda

Power Haiku

Money is power
Upper-class the wealthiest
of them rule the world.

By: Gavin Brinker
Florida, USA

<u>*Power - Haiku*</u>

Given unfairly
Not caring for powerless
Not wanting to share

Only wants endless
power, money, fame, servants
Never faced struggles

By: Christopher Persaud
Florida, USA

How we celebrate...

Songs of Kiguli

Christmas Christmas Christmas
Welcome back Christmas.
We take too long waiting for you.
We save much waiting for you.
The year can't go by without you.
Yes, we love you Christmas.

Christmas Christmas
You mean a lot to Christians.
You stay on the lips of the young.
The Son of God is born
To change our lives on earth.

Born by the power of the Holy Spirit
To Virgin Mary and Joseph,
His earthly father a carpenter,
On the 25th of December.
At Bethlehem city in a kraal,
A king was born.

The shepherds knew first
And followed the stars to the place
Where He was laid in a manger.
Herod the King heard the news,
And ordered the killing.
The Bible Says.

By: Nansereko Aisha
Uganda

Holidays! Holidays!
It is holidays again.
Every pupil gets happy.
Holidays or vacation,
People begin travelling
Up country the go to visit relatives.

Holidays! Holidays!
It's holidays again.
Most pupils enjoy holidays.
Books are kept aside.
Plenty of rest and eating while at home.

Holidays! Holidays!
It's a holiday again.
Penpals exchange letters,
Telling each other activities they've done,
Fishing, digging, or wedding.

By: Kaguta Aron
Uganda

Water as cold as ice
Indoor fire place lit up
Never ending decorations in stores
Trees covered in snow
Everywhere hot chocolate and coats
Roads packed with carolers

>By: Aijha Keith
>Florida, USA

How we have fun, the arts of our people…

Music! Music!
The sounds arranged in a pleasant way.
Music is exciting to listen to,
Regardless of age, religion or status.
The sounds are very interesting,
Leading us to another planet.

Music! Music!
It makes us dance all the time.
It touches our hearts and relaxes us.
Music makes us feel well,
All the blood vessels contain it.

Music! Music!
Music is a form of entertainment.
Giving a lot of people employment.
Making others popular and giving us hope,
Through the excitement,
Which leads a country to development.

By: Ajuma Benaleta
Uganda

Dancing! Dancing! Dancing!
When music plays,
I feel like dancing.
I nod my head.
I shake my body.

Dancing! Dancing! Dancing!
I listen to all types of music,
Traditional and pop music.
I dance all types of dances.

Through dancing I earn a living.
I get a lot of money.
Oh! I love dancing.
And I love watching those who watch my dance.

By: Narrulondo Peace
Uganda

Songs of Kiguli

Singing! Singing! Singing!
I like singing all types of songs.
I can't live without singing.
Songs which give me some advice.
Good and bad are found in songs.

Singing! Singing! Singing!
If I don't listen to music,
I feel down and not myself.
Some songs make me happy,
Because they are talking about our youth.

Singing! Singing! Singing!
I switch on the radio and music begins.
I shake my head,
I keep on dancing,
I can that sing that song.
Sometimes I get money from singing.

By: Nyangoma Shirah
Uganda

The magic in the needle,
That joins threads together.
Forming a garment,
And later becoming cloth.

The magic in the needle,
Which makes designs and fashions.
From the ready cloth,
Making shirts, skirts, trousers, etc.

The magic in the needle,
Which makes patches,
To fill in the holes created in the clothes.
Repairing the torn ones that makes cloth regain life.
There is a magic in the needle.

By: Tayebwa Keneth
Uganda

National Football League

Never has the NFL ever seen a boring moment
Follow your dreams, it may be as long as a never-ending rainbow
Leaves a huge impact in people like an amazing scar

By: Ruthnie Denais
Florida, USA

Dance

Determination to have fun while dancing
Amazing to be able to enjoy doing it
Nice people would be invited to dance
Cheerful people shine like the sun while dancing
Energetic people will dance the longest

By: Daniela Gonzalez
Florida, USA

<u>Dance - Haiku</u>

It shows our true self
I use it, shows emotion
It is happiness

By: Aniyah Hall
Florida, USA

Love Haiku

I love to sing too
Singing makes me feel happy
I was born for it

I love to eat food
Especially lasagna
I also love treats

By: Widjina Jean Giles
Florida, USA

FUN

Fun
Universal
Never-ending, like the water cycle

By: Julien Montilus
Florida, USA

How we see faith, spirituality, ourselves, and others…

World! World! World!
This world has amazing things.
All sorts of happiness and fun,
Not forgetting worries and troubles.
But, God, you are so perfect,
When crating man.
He knew all this could happen
And he had a very good plan,
A perfect friend for man.

World! World! World!
Sleep, indeed a perfect friend you are.
Man needs you after a long day of work,
To refresh the body for the next day.
Man needs you when he is worried.
You are enough to make him
Forget his worries for a while.

World! World! World!
But sometimes you are disappointing.
Especially when man needs you most
And you are not there.
You are only there when not needed.
Not only do you disturb students
Reading books, but also people
Worshiping in churches and mosques.
Not forgetting drivers on long journeys.
I wonder what king of friend you are.

By: Nakimuli Hawa
Uganda

God! God! God!
God is good all the time.
He created heaven and earth.
He made light and darkness.
He made the sun, the sky, and the rain.
They help in seeding and drying our crops.
He gave us life which we use for work.

God! God! God!
God created man in his image,
To care for His creation.

Man! Man! Man!
You disobeyed God.
You are bad. God created you in his image.
You disobeyed Him.
He gave you life.

God! God! God!
Not all people but only Adam and Eve,
Who brought problems to all people.
God told them not to eat the forbidden fruit of the tree,
Which was in the garden.
Adam and Eve brought problems like wars,
Killing of people and fighting,
Which made people to leave God.
But God should forgive people
And people should join together and praise God.

By: Mutoni Queen
Uganda

Let's get serious.
Think a little bit.
Look at your surroundings,
What do you see?
Pearls floating, glittering around you.

Rivers flowing calmly.
Blue water from the lakes.
Isolate land in lakes we call islands.
Mountains, rising and inclining.
Fish, floating in water.
Beautiful butterflies flapping their wings.
Flowers, leaves and green grass.
Wonderful nature.
Beautiful scenery.
Praises floating, glittering around you.

How I wish all the would remain,
Pearls floating forever.
But, no, this is so impossible.
Especially in the eyes of destructive citizens.
So ungrateful, never proud of their surroundings.

Our population grows day in day out.
Land is needed,
Swamps are reclaimed, forced to level ground.
All the pearls are pounded down.
Put to construction.

Oh, My God!
The effects are too harsh!
Let's get serious.
Finally, preserve our nature.
Fort it's a pearl more precious than diamonds.

By: Namonye Nathan
Uganda

Songs of Kiguli

Arise! Arise! Arise!
Rise up and shine, on the day you were born.
Very young then, very old now, with a lot to tell.

For fathers then,
High hopes they had!
Peaceful fathers then,
Curious they were.
Good seed they planted
The love for their nation, Uganda.

The plant has to grow.
The love for their country.
The plant needs care.
The love for thy country.
Tender it is.
Drop by drop it enters our heads.
Slowly, slowly the mind set will change.

Greed, revenge, and envy,
Are taking the lead.
Brotherhood is dying.
Development is failing.
The strong and the learned,
Are leaving the country.
The palm books blank with gold at their back.
Put off the mask and see what you've missed.

So let us look ahead,
Nothing to reverse,
Building our nation,
With peace and unity.

By: Namonye Nathan
Uganda

I want to drive like Uncle Michael
Zoom—Zoom—Zoom—oooooo pebecep!!

I want to bark like our dog, Simba,
Haw—Haw—Haw—

I want to meow like our old cat, Cate,
Miaow—Miaow—Miaow—Miaow

I want to talk like our deep voiced Headmaster.
"Children, today is the beginning of –"

By: Alado Bonica Teddy
Uganda

Beauty
Poem Meter Syllable count alternates 5,7, 5

Beauty everywhere
Invented by the people
Beauty is bald head
Beauty is big chops with love
Beauty hurts with tears
Enter with pride and courage
Afraid of critics
Understand Beauty inside
The Beauty's alive
Wear it everywhere

By: Sabine Bocico
Florida, USA

I Wear a Mask

I wear a mask that shows I'm kind
But no one knows what's inside my mind
I may be happy, I may be rude
But everyone say I look like a dude

By: Chinilly Brice
Florida, USA

<u>Found Poem</u>
Looks

LOOK FOR LESS!
Get the Look
for real!
for less!
Your Style

By: Shakeria Bright
Florida, USA

Determined
Energetic
Polite
Excellent all the time
Nice
Dependable
Ability
Bold
Leader
Easy Going

By: Gavin Brinker
Florida, USA

Found Poem

No situation is too risky.
He's a big strong fearless arrogant hero
Classic leader
Taking on deadly-dangerous odds instead of Dragon Rides

By: Gavin Brinker
Florida, USA

Found Poem

Top of the Heap!
tough and stubborn!
king of all
earn their status
to protect
Skullcrusher!
Ginormous Yet Gentle

the sound of your own voice and
thrive in the spotlight
the leader and always lend a
helping hand to your friends.

brave in a difficult
situation you take the helm
You like
life-threatening adventure
Except when it's to protect your friends.

Always ready to explore and learn
about your surroundings.

The may not wear any
crown
but they certainly
seek great
POWER

By: Gerald Castor
Florida, USA

Epiphany

If I had a dime for every broken promise that was made to me, would have money to last me a century.
I have an epiphany, if people do what they should do this world wouldn't be a Blues Clues, trying to find out what people mean to you, this world doesn't seem to improve. I wish I can hit the snooze.

By Gerald Castor
Florida, USA

Myself

I'm more than meets the eye, I bet you wouldn't notice me even if I cry. Who cares about that I think it's lame. I guess you can call me a little bit of a shame.

By Gerald Castor
Florida, USA

Hope

Everybody has
hope in somebody Success
not recess Have Hope

By: Emmanuel Garcia
Florida, USA

You're Amazing
Nobody perfect
We have disadvantages
We still are unique

Beauty inside us
Our beauty shines deep within
Not on the outside

By: Ruthnie Denais
Florida, USA

Humble

Yea, i am humble
I don't stumble
I show your fate
Just appreciate
Don't hate
I don't rate
I'm not fake.

By: Emmanuel Garcia
Florida, USA

Fear - Haiku

Many scary things
People have different fears.
some are crazy dumb,

But some can cause fright,
it can be fiction or real
it could be a clown

By: Daniela Gonzalez
Florida, USA

Faith

Funny
Athletics
Intelligent
Trusting
Hard working

By: Jason Hannah
Florida, USA

Haikus

Haikus are simple
But sometimes they don't make sense

By: Stephanie Joseph
Florida, USA

I wear a mask that shows
I'm mean, but what
Everyone don't know
I can be kinda keen

By: Aijha Keith
Florida, USA

<u>Faith - Haiku</u>

Have faith in yourself
Do not believe in no one
You never give up

By: Janya Martinez
Florida, USA

Found Poem
Emotion

You wake up every morning feeling neutral
When you wash your face you feel warm
and soft like the water it clouds up
in the sky blue.
The taste of your favorite cravings gives
you a mood lifting strength that makes
you feel fiery, bold, and powerful
you walk outside and can't seem
to find the feeling the grey days
of winder would give you instead
you feel the vibrancy of the
pale yellow sun in your face and
the wind that blows the earthly
green plants in the most sophisticated
way. The overwhelming feeling when
you walk into class late making your
heart pound, feeling a racy red, spicy,
emotion that slowly deepens it in
making you want to shade away behind a
bolder but when you finally come home you
feel a strong navy, cozy color in your soul.

By: Yasmine Octelus
Florida, USA

International Edition

Awkward to talk about
Demanding at the worst time
Disagreeable while sharing
Irresponsible to start
Careless
Tough as a rock

By: Christopher Persaud
Florida, USA

DISCOVER Who I am
POWER to Be a strong leader.
Extremely positive FIGHTING BACK like it's the last day on Earth
every morning I grind and shine like the Moonlight.
Travel the world and spreading. JOY ☺ around the world
Turning 15 on September 11 Happy Birthday 2017

By: Ashlyne Renelique
Florida, USA

Beauty

Beauty is beauty
Everyone is beautiful
Their own beauty way

beauty is not me
as one can see, it's beauty
ugly is beauty

By: Natalie Santisteban
Florida, USA

Found Poem

Sea Fare
FEELING BLUE A small
SEASTAR
paired with darker blues

By: Jada Wilson
Florida, USA

I Wear a Mask

I wear a mask that shows I'm funny
But also, working hard making money
Seeing bees carrying lots of honey
Having a day windy and sunny

By: Brad Sinanan
Florida, USA

Haiku Poem for Alice

Beauty is within
beauty is in everyone
beauty is the world

Fear, an emotion
Is fear a strong emotion
Fear is what we feel

loneliness is pain.
loneliness is what some feel.
loneliness is me.

By: Alyra Washington
Florida, USA

Songs of Kiguli

List of Authors in Alphabetical Order

Ajuma Benaleta, Uganda
Akankunda Justine, Uganda
Akello Faith, Uganda
Alado Bonica Teddy, Uganda
Baaty Gloria, Uganda
Bocico, Sabine, Florida, USA
Boodram, Michael, Florida, USA
Brice, Chinilly, Florida, USA
Bright, Shakeria, Florida, USA
Brinker, Gavin, Florida, USA
Castor, Gerald, Florida, USA
Cunningham, Talanya, Florida, USA
Denais, Ruthnie, Florida, USA
Garcia, Emmanuel, Florida, USA
Gonzalez, Daniela, Florida, USA
Hall, Aniyah, Florida, USA
Hannah, Jason, Florida, USA
Hatsemwa, Uganda
Hipe Martha, Uganda
Jean-Giles, Widjina, Florida, USA
Joseph, Stephanie, Florida, USA
Kabazarwe Scovia, Uganda
Kagaga Winnie, Uganda
Kaguta Aron, Uganda
Kanyesigye Herbert, Uganda
Kato Ivan, Uganda
Kawwine Grace, Uganda
Keith, Aijha, Florida, USA
Klatsernwa Merabu, Uganda
Lapyem Samuel, Uganda
Letisha Maria, Uganda

Songs of Kiguli

Mahoro Jesca, Uganda
Makubuya Rashid, Uganda
Ogwane Moses, Uganda
Mandilu James, Uganda
Maria Letisha, Uganda
Martinez, Janya, Florida, USA
Mboozi Joan, Uganda
Montilus, Julien, Florida, USA
Morris, Uganda
Mubbala Elivis, Uganda
Mukisa Remmy, Uganda
Musasizi Mike, Uganda
Mutoni Queen, Uganda
Nakimuli Hawa, Uganda
Namajja Irene, Uganda
Namonye Nathan, Uganda
Namugenyi Dorothy, Uganda
Namulando Peace, Uganda
Namulondo Sarah, Uganda
Nanajja Irene, Uganda
Nankynola Hope, Uganda
Nansereko Aisha, Uganda
Narrulondo Peace, Uganda
Nasasira Margret, Uganda
Nasazi Diana, Uganda
Naturinda Daphine, Uganda
Ndyamuhaki Elizabeth, Uganda
Noyamuhai Elizabeth, Uganda
Nyangoma Shirah, Uganda
Octelus, Yasmine, Florida, USA
Ogwane Moses, Uganda
Ohangole Johnson, Uganda

Otim Solomon, Uganda
Persaud, Christopher, Florida, USA
Powell, Rhain, Florida, USA
Renelique, Ashlyne, Florida, USA
Santisteban, Natalie, Florida, USA
Scurry, Akelye, Florida

www.ingramcontent.com/pod-product-compliance
Lightning Source LLC
Chambersburg PA
CBHW031420290426
44110CB00011B/460